Of all things considered,
nothing begins to compare
with the love that a mother
and daughter can share.

～Laurel Atherton

The Love Between a Mother and Daughter Is Forever

A Blue Mountain Arts® Collection
About the Special Bond
Mothers and Daughters Share

Special Updated Edition

Edited by Patricia Wayant

Blue Mountain Press™

Boulder, Colorado

We gratefully acknowledge the permission granted by the following authors, publishers, and authors' representatives to reprint poems or excerpts from their publications: Susan Polis Schutz for "My beautiful daughter I wish for you...," "My beautiful daughter I want you to always know...," "...a star glimmering in the sky...," "The relationship between a mother and daughter...," and "Thank You, Mom." Copyright © 1986, 1991, 1995 by Stephen Schutz and Susan Polis Schutz. All rights reserved. Sharon Riojas for "Mothers and Daughters Share a Lifelong Connection." Copyright © 2010 by Sharon Riojas. All rights reserved. *Pittsburgh Post-Gazette* for "They call each other at least..." from "Best Friends: Mothers and Daughters with the Deepest Connection" by Mackenzie Carpenter (*Pittsburgh Post-Gazette*: May 14, 2006). Copyright © 2006 by *Pittsburgh Post-Gazette*. All rights reserved. Loyola Press, www.loyolabooks.org, for "The mother-daughter relationship..." from DANCING WITH MY DAUGHTER by Jayne Jaudon Ferrer. Copyright © 2004 by Jayne Jaudon Ferrer. All rights reserved. G.P. Putnam's Sons, a division of Penguin Group (USA), Inc., for "Daughters never really leave their mothers..." from A LOTUS GROWS IN THE MUD by Goldie Hawn. Copyright © 2005 by Illume, LLC. All rights reserved. *Discovery Health*, www.health.discovery.com, for "Mother-daughter bonding can start..." from "Our Mothers, Ourselves: Mother-Daughter Relationships" by Gina Shaw (*Discovery Health*: August 2008). Copyright © 2008 by Gina Shaw. All rights reserved. HarperCollins Publishers for "At first I was just Milk Central..." and "What would I want to have written..." from SMALL WONDER by Barbara Kingsolver. Copyright © 2002 by Barbara Kingsolver. All rights reserved. And for "So what is a woman's place?" and "As I resurrect those childhood pictures..." from WE ARE OUR MOTHERS' DAUGHTERS: REVISED AND EXPANDED EDITION by Cokie Roberts. Copyright © 1998, 2000, 2009 by Cokie Roberts. All rights reserved. Harry N. Abrams, Inc., New York, for "I bless the day she came..." by Judy Swank from HOLLYWOOD MOMS by Joyce Ostin. Copyright © 2001 by Joyce Ostin. All rights reserved. *Literary Mama*, www.literarymama.com for "Mother/Daughter Day" by Andrea Potos. (*Literary Mama*: January 4, 2007). Copyright © 2007 by Andrea Potos. All rights reserved. Maria Mazziotti Gillan for "My Daughter at Fourteen: Christmas Dance" and "All my life people have expected..." from "Mothers and Daughters" from WHAT WE PASS ON: COLLECTED POEMS, 1980-2009 (Guernica Editions). Copyright © 2010 by Maria Mazziotti Gillan. All rights reserved. Debra Heintz Cavataio for "A Mother's Love Never Ends." Copyright © 2010 by Debra Heintz Cavataio. All rights reserved. Elissa Schappell for "One gray winter afternoon..." from CHILD OF MINE by Christina Baker Kline. Copyright © 1997 by Elissa Schappell. All rights reserved. BOA Editions, Ltd., www.BOAEditions.org, for "What Is Supposed to Happen" from RED SUITCASE by Naomi Shihab Nye. Copyright © 1994 by Naomi Shihab Nye. All rights reserved.

Acknowledgments are continued on the last page.

Library of Congress Control Number: 2010908827
ISBN: 978-1-59842-529-1

⊞ and Blue Mountain Press are registered in U.S. Patent and Trademark Office.
Certain trademarks are used under license.

Printed in China.
First Printing: 2010

♲ This book is printed on recycled paper.

This book is printed on paper that has been specially produced to be acid free (neutral pH) and contains no groundwood or unbleached pulp. It conforms with the requirements of the American National Standards Institute, Inc., so as to ensure that this book will last and be enjoyed by future generations.

Blue Mountain Arts, Inc.
P.O. Box 4549, Boulder, Colorado 80306

Contents

(Authors listed in order of first appearance)

Mothers
and
Daughters
Share a Lifelong
Connection

Mothers and daughters
share toddler days, teenage woes,
and grown-up joys and tears.
They grow together with tender hugs,
long goodbyes, heart-to-heart talks,
and shared dreams.
They support each other
in every aspect of life.
They express the encouragement
and comfort needed to embark
on each new challenge.
Their ongoing friendship creates
an incredible bond.
Everyone around them can see
the joy on their faces reflected
in their smiles every time
they are together.

Not much in this life endures
through all time,
but mothers and daughters
share a lifelong connection.

∾Sharon Riojas

The relationship between
a mother and daughter
is comprised of a very deep
understanding of and support for
each other
It is based on an enormous
amount of emotion and love
There is no other relationship
in the world
where two women are so much
like one

When I gave birth to
my beautiful daughter
I never knew what a
special relationship
a mother and daughter could have
As she got older
and started to understand more
about being a female
I felt as if I were going through
all the stages of growing up
once again

I felt a strong urge
to protect her from anything
that could possibly hurt her
but I knew that if I did
she would not be prepared
to face the real world
So I tried to
establish the right balance
by showing her and
explaining to her
what I consider to be
the most important things in life

And I have loved her every second
of her life
I have supported her at all times
and as her mother, as a person
and as a friend
I will always continue
to cherish and love
everything about her
my beautiful daughter

∾ Susan Polis Schutz

They call each other at least once a week, often once a day, sometimes three times a day. They trade clothes, DVDs, advice about relationships. They go shopping together, vacation together, finish each other's sentences.

They are best friends. But not the I've-known-her-since-third-grade kind.

These are best friends who are also bound together in that deepest and most profound of human connections: mothers and daughters.

∼Mackenzie Carpenter

The mother–daughter relationship — with all its twists and turns, and ups and downs, and diversity and passion and drive — is very much like a dance. We come together — for celebration, support, or commiseration; we back away — in anger or confusion, for privacy or reflection. But in one form or another, the "dance" goes on throughout our lives; we simply vary the rhythm and who gets to lead when.

∽ Jayne Jaudon Ferrer

Daughters never really leave their mothers, and thank God for that.

∽ Goldie Hawn

Mother-daughter bonding can start at an early age.

When you're five, she's a goddess. You smear your face with her lipstick and model her earrings and high heels, wanting to be just like Mommy. That's the way it is until you're about thirteen, when she suddenly becomes the most ignorant, benighted, out-of-touch creature on the planet, and you can't get far enough away from her. Your primary form of interaction for the next five years or so will be a single word, "Mooooooooooooommmmmmm!" And then, somewhere between your twenties and your thirties, if you're lucky, she becomes your best friend again.

∽Gina Shaw

At first I was just Milk Central, then tiptoe walking coach and tea-party referee. Eventually I began to see that the common denominator, especially as mother of a girl child, was to protect and value every part of your personality and will, even when it differed from mine.

∽Barbara Kingsolver

I don't recall the first time
    my mother held me
or when I first heard her voice.
But from the first moment
    she held me in her arms,
she made the most selfless choice.

She chose to change her busy life
so that my life could begin.
She was my shelter from the rain;
on her, I could depend.

She held my hand when I was afraid
and helped me to mend my first broken heart.
She bandaged my wounds, wiped my tears,
and kept me from falling apart.

She loved me without question,
    no matter what I did.
She shaped me into a confident adult
    from such an awkward kid.

Even though she's not always
    right beside me,
her love is matched by no other.
And I am so thankful every day
for this wonderful gift... my mother.

∽ Stacey Swayze

A Daughter Is One of Life's Greatest Blessings

A daughter begins her life loving and trusting
   you automatically
and for many years, you are the center of her life
Together you experience the delights of
   the new things she learns and does
You enter into her play and are once again young
And even though it's harder to enter into her
   world as she becomes a teen
you are there, understanding her dilemmas and
   her fears
and wishing with all your heart that she didn't
   have to go through them
Her successes mean more to you than your own
and her happiness is your happiness
Words can't express how much she means to you —
the love goes too deep, and the gratitude
   and pride are boundless
In so many ways, she is life's greatest blessing

∽Barbara Cage

I bless the day she came to me...
My little girl with the big brown eyes.
Through the years
she made me laugh so hard I cried.
She shared her dreams.
She shared her heart.
We shared the risks.
We share our love.
And she taught me courage to find my way.
What beautiful, joyful moments we have had —
me and my little girl with the big brown eyes.

∽ Judy Swank

Mother/Daughter Day

After a rare no school day:
the coffeeshop, the Harry Potter matinee,
home for spaghetti and meatballs,
she hugs my waist to tell me
she loves the mother/daughter day,
words I hold, like the piece of her first haircut,
snipped coils of auburn light inside my dresser,
beside the two kindergarten teeth I smuggled
from the tooth fairy one night.

I'll stash them against the thunder
everyone claims is coming — five or six years
from here when she'll look at me as if I'm from
Mars or some errant moon, tearing herself apart
from me like the perforated edges of the Madeline
paper dolls she and I once dressed and undressed
before tucking them in their toyroom beds.

∽ Andrea Potos

My Daughter at Fourteen: Christmas Dance

Panic in your face, you write questions
to ask him. When he arrives,
you are serene, your fear
unbetrayed. How unlike me you are.

After the dance,
I see your happiness; he holds
your hand. Though you barely speak,
your body pulses messages I can read

all too well. He kisses you goodnight,
his body moving toward yours, and yours
responding. I am frightened, guard my
tongue for fear my mother will pop out

of my mouth. "He is not shy," I say. You giggle,
a little girl again, but you tell me he
kissed you on the dance floor. "Once?"
I ask. "No, a lot."

We ride through rain-shining 1 a.m.
streets. I bite back words which long
to be said, knowing I must not shatter your
moment, fragile as a spun-glass bird,

you, the moment, poised on the edge of
flight, and I, on the ground, afraid.

∽Maria Mazziotti Gillan

A Mother's Love
Never Ends

A mother holds her daughter so close to her heart. With intuition and the strongest love, she finds a way to nurture, protect, and guide her through life. She has no real idea how fast the time will pass by. She looks back on every day and tries to hold on to those cherished moments that seem to slip away so quickly.

Then comes the time in her life when she realizes her daughter is all grown up. Now she must step back and let her child go on alone, as she watches from a distance. She remembers the years that came and went so quickly and realizes just how deeply blessed her life has been. She misses the child she used to know but looks forward to the future. She feels proud of the person she has raised; she feels complete as a person. But more than anything else, she feels honored to be called "Mother."

∾Debra Heintz Cavataio

I have shared a relationship with my mother since the moment I was born. The bond between us is enormous, and sometimes frustrating, but it's something I can always count on when it feels as if everything else is falling apart.

I'm so glad that God in His infinite wisdom allowed me to belong to her — to be her child and her friend. More than anything, I'm so thankful to have been given the honor to love her and call her my mother.

∽ Pamela Malone-Melton

One gray winter afternoon... [my baby daughter, Isadora] was teething and was in an uncharacteristically cranky mood. I had a crushing headache and hadn't slept well the night before, so we were a very unhappy pair.... Feeling helpless, I put a Nina Simone CD on the stereo, one I'd listened to a lot while pregnant. I held Isadora in my arms, her chest against mine, one arm wrapped around my neck, her other held out to the side, her fist enfolded in my palm. I started to sway with her, not rocking, but dancing. She held her head up, and for the first time all day smiled back at me. I wondered if she remembered the music from the womb. I spun slowly in a circle, and dipped her. She laughed, and even though she'd laughed before, this was the most beautiful and surprising sound I'd ever heard.... The day's anxiety fled my body at her touch. I felt like she belonged to me — like I was truly her mother. Felt like this moment alone with her, each of us comforting the other, was sacred.

∽Elissa Schappell

I think my life began with waking up and loving my mother's face.

∽Mary Ann Evans (George Eliot)

What Is Supposed to Happen

When you were small,
we watched you sleeping,
waves of breath
filling your chest.
Sometimes we hid behind
the wall of baby, soft cradle
of baby needs.
I loved carrying you between
my own body and the world.

Now you are sharpening pencils,
entering the forest of
lunch boxes, little desks.
People I never saw before
call out your name
and you wave.

This loss I feel,
this shrinking,
as your field of roses
grows and grows....

Now I understand history.
Now I understand my mother's
ancient eyes.

∽Naomi Shihab Nye

A Daughter Always Needs Her Mom

No matter how old I get,
I'll still need to hear my mother say
she's proud of me.
I'll need her advice,
even though I may not take it.
I'll need to know how she is —
even when she doesn't feel well
or would rather not "burden" me
with her problems.
No matter how busy I get,
I'll always need to hear her say
she thought of me today.
I'll need to hear her voice,
even if I may not have
enough time to talk.
I still need to know she loves me.

No matter how upset I am,
I'll always need to hear her say
that she knows I can handle it.
I'll still need to hear
her honest opinion,
even though it might annoy me.
I'll want to know about
her experiences,
even if it takes me years
to learn from them
or apply them to my own situations.
No matter what's going on in my life...
I will always need my mom.

~ Gail Dickert

Even now, my first thought is to call Mom
whenever something big happens,
good or bad.
I still need her reassurance.
I still like to share my triumphs with her,
and I still need to hear her loving voice.
I am so thankful
there is someone in the world
who thinks I am indispensable,
cheers me on,
and loves me unconditionally.
People never really outgrow their moms...
I know I never will.

∽Kelly Maureen Paquet

To the Strongest Soul I Know...
My Mom

I look to you for strength and courage.
I look to you for moral guidance.
You have always been the captain
of my one-person cheer squad,
and your devotion has never wavered.
When I was uncertain
and afraid I had let you down,
you showed no disappointment.
You were proud of me
simply because I had done my best.
Your strength shone through
my weakest moments,
allowing me to find the answers
at my own pace.
You are the strongest soul I know,
and I am strong because of you.
Your support is unchanged
and only reinforces our bond.
Mother and daughter is how we began,
but today I consider you
my one true best friend.

∽Nicole Cook

A Mother Finds a Special Friend in a Daughter

When my daughter was young, it seemed as if
I was constantly busy taking care of her and trying
to keep up with the demands of raising a child.
In time, it seemed as if our roles somehow became reversed,
and she returned my devotion
by letting me lean on her.
There were times when she seemed
so wise for her years that I caught a glimpse of the woman
she would someday become.
Now she is my dearest friend —
one who is loving, kind, and compassionate.
She supports me at all times by giving her time and love;
I know I can count on her to always be there.
She listens to my problems
with quiet understanding, and through her
I am often able to find solutions.
She is my biggest fan
when I have achieved a personal goal,
sharing my triumphs with pride and affection.
I love her because she is my daughter,
but I also love her for the very special person she is.

∽Lori Pike

As mother and daughter,
we've always been like best friends.
We don't take each other for granted;
we don't demand that we be
anything more than who we are.
We accept the fact that sometimes
we aren't exactly the way
we wish we could be.
We have always believed in each other,
and I think that is what will always be
the strongest part of our relationship.
Because of who we are,
we not only appreciate, respect,
and trust each other,
we also have the opportunity
to learn how to value
each other's uniqueness.
I am forever thankful for
the loving and caring relationship
we have as mother and daughter
and as truly the best of friends.

∽Laura Medley

Even when my daughter was just a little girl, there were times when our relationship tended to be more about friendship than mother and daughter things. We enjoyed many of the same activities and could laugh about the absurd and silly situations until our sides ached. She was often the one to make me see another side of an issue and to cause me to change my attitude when it was wrong.

∽Barbara Cage

I love that I can talk with her about anything... serious or light. And I love that we can laugh together, not only as mother and daughter, but as friends.

∽Debbie Burton-Peddle

To My Incredible Daughter

I love being your mother. You are your own person, and I get to see what you choose to do with your time and talents. You may have started small and helpless in my arms, but now I know you are capable of so much. It has inspired me to watch you grow brilliantly into yourself. I have always had such high hopes for you, and you continue to exceed them with the incredible person you are.

When I look at you, I see years of memories and decades of potential. You have already changed my world in spectacular ways, and now I see you impact the rest of the world in wonderful ways as well. I am honored to be your mother.

∽Amy L. Kuo

Through the Eyes
of a Daughter

When I stopped seeing my mother with the eyes
of a child, I saw the woman who helped me give
birth to myself.

~ Nancy Friday

I am so proud of my mother
for the life she's lived
and the example she's been to me.
No matter the situations life has dealt,
she's handled them with honor and grace.
She is a woman of countless abilities.
I've looked up to her all my life;
growing up, I assumed she could do most anything.
She is kind, caring, dependable, and wise.
I have a mom who makes me so proud!

~ Cheryl Barker

When I look at my mother, I see my life through her eyes. I see the strength she always offers me, the comfort she continuously shows me, the support she provides me, and the magnitude of the love that she unselfishly shares.

I see the tears she sheds when I cry, the laughter she shares when I laugh, the hope she has for me when I feel disillusioned, and the faith she has in me when I face life's challenges.

I see the many sacrifices she has made and continues to make for me, the inspiration she is to me when I need direction, the devotion she shows to me as a parent, and the encouragement she gives to me when I need a friend.

When I look at my mother and see my life through her eyes, I feel very loved, fortunate, and blessed.

∽Susan Hickman Sater

It Means So Much to Be Your Daughter

As a child, I played tea party
with my baby dolls
and dreamt up imaginary people
and conversations.

As I grew older, I revealed my secrets
in the whispers and giggles of sleepovers
and, as an adult,
over late-night drinks with college friends.

I've had so many friends throughout
the years who have helped shape
a little part of me
and left me with some fond memories.

But my mother has remained
the permanent fixture in my life,
the one who knows the complete
and complicated me.

It is her patience and guidance,
her true and lasting companionship,
that have taught me how to be
a good friend to so many others.

～Kayla Washko

I love it when people tell me,
"You're just like your mom,"
because I think my mom is the most
amazing woman in the world.
I feel so totally blessed
to be her daughter,
and I know nothing will ever
change the bond we share.

All my life, I've watched her
selflessly put others first,
and I hope she knows how much
I appreciate the sacrifices she's made
to enrich my life.

She truly is the kindest,
most caring woman I've ever known,
and no matter where life takes me
I'll always be proud to call her my mom.

Whenever people say I resemble her,
I receive it as the greatest compliment of all.
For I know she is the most beautiful
woman in the world,
and I'll spend the rest of my life
aspiring to be just like her...
inside and out.

∽ Peggy Morris

What a Mother Sees

When I look at my daughter, I see someone who
has the courage and strength to overcome many
obstacles. I see someone who has a big heart and
who touches so many lives without even knowing it.
I see someone who has been blessed with not only
outer beauty but inner beauty — the kind of beauty
that is everlasting.

∽Mary Adisano

I see my heritage in her,
but the best part is her individuality —
the smile that's hers alone,
her precious personality,
her amazing creativity,
and her beauty within
that touches the world
with the wonder of who she is.

∽Barbara J. Hall

One little look inside my heart,
    Daughter,
is all you'd need
to see that my love for you
shines in every part of me
and touches all that is there.
If you took a second glance,
you'd quickly see how proud
I am of the person you've become.
Thinking of how you've grown
    and changed
makes me misty-eyed
as joy and nostalgia sweep
    through me.
If you looked a little closer,
you'd also see my support,
    love, and concern for you.
There you have it —
a peek into my heart
and a look at my love for you.

                          ∽ Cheryl Barker

A Mother and Her Girls

[My daughters have] learned from each other's strengths and weaknesses and from mine (my weaknesses are, of course, one of their great bonds in frustration as well as amusement). The older one has toughened the other; the younger one demonstrates a nonconforming streak that impresses, and even inspires, the older one. We are loyal; we like dim sum; we don't mix our metals; we don't tolerate prejudice. We share a sense of humor that is all raised eyebrows and storytelling and neither puns nor jokes (we do actually have four jokes between us, two of which are funny). They dress me now, these tall, breathtaking young women, more than I (am allowed to) dress them, and the younger one says, having picked out my shoes, "You're pretty." And the older one says, admiring her handiwork (and rolling her eyes at my choice of necklace), "Yeah, you're cute." And I know that we all are seeing our same pieces refracted and placed differently on three women, all partially dressed in each other's clothes, all held in each other's eyes, and each one created, in part, by the other two.

⌒ Amy Bloom

For me, being a mother of girls has softened me up in such a great way. I feel so honored to be a mother of girls. I grew up with a sister and I'm extremely close with my mom and her sisters....

It's so nice to be soft and girlie with these precious little girls. It's been really nice.

∾Rebecca Romijn

Becoming a mother, having a girl, has helped me love the girl I am. I may no longer have the prestige, the power, or the money that comes from succeeding in the boy's world. But I am a mother. A mother of daughters. And this is more.

∾Martha Brockenbrough

Famous
Mothers and Daughters

◌ Anne Boleyn and Queen Elizabeth I of England

◌ Blythe Danner and Gwyneth Paltrow

◌ Debbie Reynolds and Carrie Fisher

◌ Diane Ladd and Laura Dern

◌ Goldie Hawn and Kate Hudson

◌ Hillary Clinton and Chelsea Clinton

- Ingrid Bergman and Isabella Rossellini

- Ivana Trump and Ivanka Trump

- Janet Leigh and Jamie Lee Curtis

- Jayne Mansfield and Mariska Hargitay

- Joan Rivers and Melissa Rivers

- Judy Garland and Liza Minnelli

- Mary Wollstonecraft and Mary Shelley

- Maureen O'Sullivan and Mia Farrow

- Naomi Judd and Wynonna and Ashley Judd

- Priscilla Presley and Lisa Marie Presley

- Sharon Osbourne and Kelly Osbourne

- Tippi Hedren and Melanie Griffith

- Vanessa Redgrave and Natasha Richardson

Like Mother,
like Daughter

As is the mother, so is her daughter.

∾Ezekiel 16:44 (KJV)

Mothers of daughters are daughters of mothers and have remained so, in circles joined to circles, since time began. They are bound together by a shared destiny.

∾Signe Hammer

I am my mother's daughter...
instilled with a sense of family so great that nothing could break that bond and nothing could ever come before it.

I am my mother's daughter...
inheriting her strength and compassion for one and all, giving heart and soul to family, friends, and strangers.

I am my mother's daughter...
infused with sparkling energy to take care of my home, work, family, and friends. I give each the single-minded focus they need.

I am my mother's daughter...
and there is no other daughter I would want to be. My mother has shown me the way to be a strong, compassionate person by being the perfect example of one herself. And living life knowing that I am just like her makes me proud to be truly me.

∽Nicole Sullivan

A Team of Two

When the nurse brought my baby in, I looked into her face and saw myself — her eyes, her skin, her expressions, her spirit. She looked up at me and smiled her first hello.... Wynonna and I were instantly one, a partnership, a team — just the two of us against a frightening and unknown world. On that spring day... we began our wonderful duet, a blend of heart, mind, and soul that continues to this day.

∾Naomi Judd

We all hope to feel our mother's arm around our shoulders when we're worried, to feel it gently let go when life calms down. It's an intricate duet that moms and daughters dance — one backing off when the other needs space, moving up close when the unfamiliar threatens.

∾Cathie Kryczka

In my growing-up years,
we went through so much together
    as a team.
My mom made my life her own,
sacrificing her happiness for mine.
She never gave up on me.
She simply stood by me,
reassuring me that I would make it
through any obstacle that came my way.
There were times when tears filled my eyes
and I was filled with doubt,
but during those times when I was most fragile,
she was the steady rock that kept me from
    falling apart.
She was so strong and loving,
so sweet and kind.
I truly don't know
what I would do without her.

                       ~ Shannon M. Dickinson

The Sunshine and the Rain

We haven't always agreed on everything... whether it's been food, fad, or fashion, but I think it's natural for mothers and daughters to think differently. As a mother, it's easy to come from a place of feeling "right" much of the time. Sometimes it's difficult for a mother to let go and realize that she may not have all the answers and that her daughter has found some of her own along the way.

∽Kathryn Leibovich

Even as a little girl, she had a clear sense of self with her own original approach and strong resolve. And she still has the same unique style. We have not always agreed with each other, but then what mother and daughter do? Looking back, I have to say that I have always secretly admired her spirited responses. She has never been afraid to show her true colors.

∽ Lynda Field

If my mother hadn't interfered and let me know when I did things that were wrong... If she had allowed me to make decisions that I wasn't old enough to make on my own... If she never opened her ears and listened when I had something to say... If I had never had a mother, like her, who cared enough to set me straight when I needed it... I wouldn't be the person I am today.

∽T. L. Nash

A Special Connection...

Some moms have the ability
to really connect with their daughters —
to see them and sense who they are
and what they need.
Some moms are able simply to look
at their daughters
and know what's really going on.
They have that "mom sense"
that develops from spending time
with their daughters
and paying extra-close attention.
I'm lucky I have a mom with "mom sense,"
a mom who knows just how I'm feeling
and who I really am.
Having a mother who takes the time
to get to know her daughter
is a true gift.

∽ Mia Geiger

. . .an Unbreakable Bond

The moment I held her in my arms, I became
a different person. You could say that I joined
the human race. For the first time in my life, my
connection with someone else sliced through the
web of defenses, fear, and pride that had separated
me from the world.... This tiny baby became the
center of my world.

~Susan Cheever

All the little things
we've been through
and all the big things we've faced
have made our relationship
what it is today:
a bond that's stronger than ever.
There aren't enough words
to express how much I love you,
what you mean to me,
and how blessed I feel to have
    you in my life.

~Linda E. Knight

The Magic of Family

Family is a bridge across time and space to places that seem far away — but are always as close as your mind can see and your heart can hear. People in a family can reach out to each other anytime, anyplace — they can span oceans with their smiles.

No matter where you are or where they are, when you think of each other there is an instant connection and a sharing of feelings that are deep, real, and freely expressed. You share a life full of special reminiscences where just opening a family photo album or scrapbook can bring back the good times. There are customs and traditions to preserve your family ties, and there is a family spirit, alive and well, wherever good feelings dwell. Family is held in your heart forever.

~ Jacqueline Schiff

Family is a feeling of
belonging and acceptance.
It's a safe retreat, a shelter,
and an instant connection
to the people who have faith in you —
a wonderful circle of lifelong friends
whose smiles go straight
to your heart with love.
It's a special source of well-being —
full of people who hold you
     in the roughest times,
share your life,
and love to be there for you.

∽ Barbara J. Hall

No matter what life brings my way
or how my life changes from year to year,
I will always have love in my heart
and the feelings of family
to make my life worthwhile.

∽Ben Daniels

A Mother Is Always There for Her Daughter

From the time I was born,
my mother has always been there for me —
    my source of warmth and comfort,
    my greatest encouragement,
    my biggest fan,
    my confidante,
    my best and truest friend.

            ∽ Helen Vincent

If she hadn't been there to support
and encourage me, I might not have
grown up to be the confident
person I am.

            ∽ Marlo Thomas

My beautiful daughter
I want you to always know that
in good and in bad times
I will love you
and that no matter what you do
or how you think
or what you say
you can depend on
my support, guidance
friendship and love
every minute of every day
I love being your mother

∾ Susan Polis Schutz

A Woman's Strength

Women have strengths that amaze men.
They carry children, they carry hardships,
    they carry burdens —
but they hold happiness, love, and joy.
They smile when they want to scream.
They sing when they want to cry.
They cry when they are happy and laugh
    when they are nervous.
They fight for what they believe in.
They stand up to injustice.
They are in the front row at PTA meetings.
They don't take "no" for an answer when they believe
    there is a better solution.
They go without new shoes so their children can
    have them.
They go to the doctor with a frightened friend.
They love unconditionally.

They cry when their children excel
   and cheer when their friends get awards.
They are happy when they hear about a birth
   or a new marriage.
Their hearts break when a friend dies.
They have sorrow at the loss of a family member,
   yet they are strong when they think there is no
      strength left.
They know that a hug and a kiss can heal
   a broken heart.
Women come in all sizes, in all colors and shapes.
They'll drive, fly, walk, run, or e-mail you
   to show how much they care about you.
The heart of a woman is what makes the world spin!
Women do more than just give birth —
they bring joy and hope,
they give compassion and ideals,
they give moral support to their family and friends.
Women have a lot to say and a lot to give.

∽ Author Unknown

Mothers and Daughters Light the World with Their Love

Mothers and daughters
are two separate worlds
getting to know each other better.
Laughing together, being silly,
trying on each other's heart —
mothers and daughters are
a celebration of living.
They are there for each other
as they go through the ups,
downs, and in-betweens —
and they thrive.

Mothers and daughters have
open arms for each other,
the perfect recipe for a happy family,
and all the fun you can bake into a day.
They are everyday treasures
who grow more beautiful through time.
Who can imagine a world
without mothers and daughters?
They are each other's star,
lighting the world with their love.

∾Linda E. Knight

All my life people have expected me to be strong,
to carry them like sacks on my back,
to juggle several lives in my hands
without dropping anything. "Amazing,"
they said, "How do you manage?"
and I kept on going.
Only my mother was stronger than me,
who always thought of myself as weak
and small by comparison,
until she died
and I had to step into her shoes
and was shocked to find how well they fit me.

Tonight, driving home from my father's house,
I realize that only my daughter lets me lean on her,
so when she walks into the house, it is as though she carries
a bright light with her, and I can feel my straight spine
relaxing, the tension leaving my body
so quickly I imagine I can hear it,
the way I can hear air being let out of a tire.

When I know she's coming home, all day I am happy
thinking of her sharp wit, her laugh,
the way we share so much.

∽ Maria Mazziotti Gillan

So what is a woman's place? For most women it's many places, different places at different times. For almost all women, it's the place of nurturer, whether for the planet or one small creature on it. We learned it from our mothers, both in word and in deed; we teach it to our daughters in the knowledge that they must carry on the culture and care for it. Even as they go forward in this new millennium, knowing things we never knew, they will be connected back to those women in Marathon, Greece. From that continuity they will derive the strength to make their place wherever they think it should be.

∽ Cokie Roberts

A Mother's Lullaby

"Somewhere over the rainbow..."
she sings to me softly,
rocking back and forth
on her brown rocking chair.

I look into her caring blue eyes
with tears beginning to fill them
watching, simply watching
her baby girl... me,
falling fast asleep.

Her arms wrapped around me
so warm.
Her baby girl,
so many years later...
Still I lay my head in her lap,
with tears running down my face,
streaming onto my lips
the saltiness... the taste I can barely grip.

I tell her what's wrong,
about issues and things going on.

She pauses
waiting, simply waiting
for my sobs to cease.
I look into her eyes,
her caring, soft blue eyes.

It is then she sighs
and begins to sing,
"Somewhere over the rainbow..."

And once again,
as she did back then,
she begins to cry.
This sweet, soft-spoken song,
a mother's lullaby.

∾ Rachel Carrere

A Mother Is. . .

...a guiding light who holds all the ladders that reach
to your stars and catches you every time you fall.

∽ Laurel Atherton

...someone who encourages your dreams,
applauds your accomplishments,
understands your mistakes,
and is always, always proud of you.

∽ Anna Marie Edwards

...the guardian angel of the family, the queen,
the tender hand of love. A mother is the best
friend anyone ever has. A mother is love.

∽ Author Unknown

A Daughter Is...

...a star glimmering in the sky
   a wonder, a sweetness
   a perception, a delight...
   everything beautiful
   A daughter is love

       ∾ Susan Polis Schutz

    ...the essence of joy and the true meaning
      of life, the part of you that you're most
      proud of, love—endless and pure.

         ∾ Linda Sackett-Morrison

...one of the most beautiful gifts
   this world has to give.

      ∾ Laurel Atherton

How Quickly the Time Passes

How quickly she went from a sweet, innocent baby to a silly, cute toddler... and now she is a beautiful and charming woman!

I never dreamed that time would go by so quickly, but just look at what happened — my daughter blossomed into a lovely and independent young lady before I was even ready. I am so lucky to have had the luxury of seeing her go through all the little changes a child experiences as she ventured down the fast road to adulthood. All those wonderful memories of her back then are still fresh in my heart today. The tears, the scraped knees, the special friends, the first kiss... I appreciate each phase of those tender years.

∽ Dianne Cogar

At first you take care of your daughter's every need, but gradually this shifts as she grows up. First you carry her in a backpack; soon she's walking on her own. Abruptly, during the teen years, it seems as if she doesn't need you at all anymore. You're no longer your daughter's life source as she pushes for more independence. Painful as it is to go through, that's the way it's meant to be. It's your sacred duty to give your daughter roots to support her and wings to fly.

∽ Judy Ford

The years hold precious memories, but most of all, they hold growth. In a way, we grew up together.

∽ Susan M. Pavlis

For My Grown-Up Daughter

From the very second
they placed you in my arms
on the day you were born
and you turned those
trusting eyes to me,
I knew our relationship
as mother and daughter
would be extraordinary.

From the beginning,
we shared a kindred spirit.
Over the years, we mingled
our joy with giggles
and sorrow with tears.
Through it all,
we became even closer.

Your optimistic outlook on life
is one of your most endearing qualities.
It has lifted my soul numerous times
and quieted my fears just as often.

Sometimes people think the mother
is the stronger one
because she has lived longer.
I disagree.
I see your strength;
you live out your beliefs
and hold strong to your bright hopes
for the future.

You have become an amazing woman,
and I look forward to spending
many more wonderful times together.

∿ Linda C. Tuttle

What My Mother Has Given to Me

I have all the warmth of home in every corner of my heart and soul. I have encouragement to fulfill all the potential of my talents and the dreams I sincerely desire to make real.

I have a super role model of character, values, and ethical standards to guide me in all my relationships and decision making. I have the inner strength to stand up for my convictions and live according to my own design. I have the courage to rise to the challenges in my life.

I have the daring to assert my right to be my best and brightest. I have my dreams and the will to reach them. I have all the skills to depend on myself for health, happiness, and success. I have a spirit of adventure, imagination, and creativity.

I have customs and traditions that nestle me securely in my heritage and shine for me with all the light of family. I have pride in my history and in the people who blazed a trail so that I could achieve my own kind of greatness. I have an appreciation for the past and a passion for shaping the future.

I have happiness to call my own and a thankfulness that accompanies every thought of her. I have a friendship full of genuine loyalty, laughter, and love. Because of my mom, I have it all — and nothing in the world means more to me.

∽ Jacqueline Schiff

For a Daughter Who Leaves

A woman weaves
her daughter's wedding
slippers that will carry
her steps into a new life.
The mother weeps alone
into her jeweled sewing box
slips red thread
around its spool,
the same she used to stitch
her daughter's first silk jacket
embroidered with turtles
that would bring luck, long life.
She remembers all the steps
taken by her daughter's
unbound quick feet:
dancing on the stones
of the yard among yellow
butterflies and white-breasted sparrows.
And she grew, legs strong
body long, mind
independent.

Now she captures all eyes
with her hair combed smooth
and her hips gently
swaying like bamboo.
The woman
spins her thread
from the spool of her heart,
knotted to her daughter's
departing
wedding slippers.

∾Janice Mirikitani

How lonely the house seems — I never knew before how well you helped to fill it.... Ever since you went away, I have been wondering if it was as hard for you to go out into the world as it was for me to have you go.

∽ Florence Wenderoth Saunders

Letting go is not easy. But when I look at my daughter now — a beautiful young woman, strong in her convictions and determined to face life on her own terms — I feel my heart swell with pride and joy...

In one simple truth: even though her hand may slip away from mine, we will hold each other in our hearts forever.

∽ Nancy Gilliam

My Daughter
Is a Mother

It seems just like yesterday
that I held you in my arms
    for the first time,
and now here you are — a mother
with a child of your own.

～Charlene Straznitskas

Mothers and daughters are closest
when daughters become mothers.

～Author Unknown

Now that you're a mother, you see how easy it was for me to love you — and how life changes for the better the day you are blessed with a child. Now you feel all the happiness I felt on the day you were born.

As a mother, you understand that the little eyes that look into yours can give you hope for a wonderful tomorrow, and the tiniest hand can take you to the greatest places on earth and lead you to life's true happiness.

I learned all this the day you took your first breath. In that moment of my life, I realized that I was about to take my first breath, too. Everything I needed that day was wrapped in a tiny blanket and placed next to my heart — where you have grown and blossomed into a beautiful and amazing woman.

Now I can stand back and smile as I watch my most precious gift — you, my daughter — experience the wonderful blessing of being... a mother.

∽ Debra Heintz Cavataio

Two Hearts Filled with Pride

When my daughter was young,
I thought of her future life.
Perhaps she would fly to the moon
or, if not, at least land on a star.
I knew she could do whatever
she set her mind to.
I saw her as a leader,
strong in her convictions,
able to move mountains,
not just for herself,
but for others also.
I am so proud of her,
of the woman she has become
with all her effort and hard work.
I hope she can feel
the warm love I have for her always.

∽ Carol Lawson

Mom, you always told me that I could be
anything I wanted to be.
You told me I was intelligent, creative, full of talent,
and that no matter what I wanted to do,
I would be able to do it.

But what about you?
Has anyone ever told you
how wonderful you really are?
How the love in your eyes,
the tenderness in your voice,
the soft, comforting touch of your hands
have healed more wrongs
than any team of specialists could ever heal?
That the place you have created, our home,
is warm and full of life and love?
Has anyone ever thanked you
for the love and the care
you put into the hours of everyday life?

Those are special gifts and special talents.
They are not something that
you can be taught in school.
They are gifts of love,
gifts that I hope to possess someday
and to be able to share with my family.

∽ Lea Walsh

A Lifetime of Memories

As I resurrect those childhood pictures in my memory, they all include Mamma. To me, she was the most beautiful woman on earth, and she seemed a constant presence. When I was little I used to fake being sick so I could stay home and play with her. She knew what I was doing, but never let on. Now I realize how many cancellations and rearrangements must have followed in the wake of my announcements that I didn't feel quite up to going to school that day.

∾Cokie Roberts

You never realize how much your mother loves you till you explore the attic — and find every letter you ever sent her, every finger painting, clay pot, bead necklace, Easter chicken, cardboard Santa Claus, paperlace Mother's Day card, and school report since day one.

∾Pam Brown

Time and time again, I am reminded of
what the power of a mother's love can do.
My mother has seen the "real me,"
and yet somehow still thinks
　　of me as someone special;
she's known me at my worst
and yet her caring never loses
　　any of its strength.
She has the ability to put herself
　　in my shoes
even if it's a tight squeeze
and the know-how to keep me pointed
　　in the right direction.
There's a special tie between us
that grows more beautiful
　　through the years —
with memories, like ribbons,
that will forever keep us close at heart.

　　　　　　　　∽Linda E. Knight

She'll Always Be
My Little Girl

There was a time when she needed me to dress her, comb her hair, and kiss the hurt away. Today, those times are just lingering memories — and I wonder where the years went. If I'd known they would end so soon, I'd have held her a little longer, kissed her more, and told her more often just how much I love her.

I'm thankful for the woman she's become, and I take pride in the fact that I had a hand in it. But she still is and will always be my little girl.

∼ Machella D. Fisher

I miss those days when she spoke her first words,
took her first cautious steps,
and love and caring were all she needed.
I thought she would always be my baby,
and in a way, she is.
But as she has grown, so has my love for her.

∼ Joanna Naso

Occasionally I still see
the little girl in her
and realize that some things
    never change.

It may be just the way
she turns her head
or a certain look in her eyes...
but in that instant I'm reminded
that this woman is still my little girl.

～Cheryl Barker

A daughter may outgrow your lap,
but she will never outgrow your heart.

～Author Unknown

Apart but Still So Close

Though we're not always together,
we always have a strong, warm,
and forever feeling of togetherness.
It's there in our lives, welcoming us
just as surely as the sun coming up
in the morning, and just as certain
as the stars that shine above.

I think that feeling is such a beautiful
reflection of the wonderful bond we
share, and it says so much about the
remarkable and thankful things that
two caring souls are capable of.

Being a mother and a daughter
has a lot to do with the deepest
and sweetest feelings in the heart...

And with always being together,
even when you have to be apart.

～ S. J. Ellenson

Dearest of feelings,
sweetest of friends,
sharing such closeness,
joy without end.

Caring about each other
all our lives through,
the thankfulness of me
and the beauty of you.

In all our days,
in both our hearts,
there is never a time
when our thoughts are apart.

Of all things considered,
nothing begins to compare
with the love that a mother
and daughter can share.

∽ Laurel Atherton

Mother and daughter. The relationship that encompasses a gallery of emotions the depth and power of which is found in no other.

Mothers and daughters.

Keepers of the flame, the faith, the family.

Like different sides of the same coin, they are each other's mirror, each other's looking glass, each other's reflection.

Because in the end a mother knows what no woman who has not raised a child could possibly know: her children, her daughters, will learn from her the power and the magic of courage, of strength, and, ultimately, of a mother's love.

༄Laura B. Randolph

My Mother, My Mirror

Every once in a while, I look in the mirror
and right there in front of me
    I see you staring back.
I guess it's true...
the nut doesn't fall far from the tree!
There's no denying it...
you're in my face... in my laugh...
    in everything I do.

And you know what?
I wouldn't have it any other way.
You taught me to enjoy life,
to see the best in others,
    and to laugh at myself.
The best part is you will always be with me.

Whenever I am missing you,
I can just look in the mirror.
I'll see you smiling back at me,
and we can laugh ourselves silly,
    just like we always have!

                    ∾Suzy Toronto

These Are Our
Prayers and Wishes
as Mother and Daughter

That we may always be more than close.
That nothing will come
    between the bond of love we share.
That I will always be there for you,
    as you will be for me.
That we will listen with love.
That we will share truths and
    tenderness.
That we will trust and talk things out.
That we will understand.
That wherever you go, you will be
    in my heart,
and your hand will be in my hand.

∽ Laurel Atherton

Throughout the day, Daughter, I offer little prayers that things are going well for you... that you have what you need... that you're smiling and laughing and keeping company with friends... that you are safe and comfortable and enjoying your life. Most of all, I pray you feel my love within your heart for this moment and always.

∾ Linda Sackett-Morrison

If a star were to fall in the sky tonight... and I could make a wish... the one thing I would ask for is that my mother never forget that she's the best mother there is.

She's helped me hold on to so many memories of our special yesterdays, and she's helped me touch tomorrow... just by loving me and encouraging me to go after my hopes and dreams and do what I can to make them come true.

She has given me the perfectly precious gift of her love, which I value more highly than any treasure on this earth.

∾ Anna Tafoya

What would I want to have written on stone? Not to complete some national agenda, but just for *us*?....

My daughters, as precious as my eyes: I would have them be brave enough, and gentle enough, to remember me by embracing the world and engaging in its design. I wouldn't need to know how they'd do it, only that they would earn the unquenchable happiness that comes to those who leave a place more beautiful, somehow, for their having walked through it.

∿Barbara Kingsolver

A mother wishes
for her daughter to always see
    the goodness in this world,
to do her part in helping those
    less fortunate,
to find her special purpose
    in this world so full of choices.

∿Jackie Olson

My beautiful daughter
I wish for you to have
    people to love
    people in your life who will care about you
        as much as I do
    blue skies and clear days
    exciting things to do
    easy solutions to any problems
    knowledge to make the right decisions
    strength in your values
    laughter and fun
    goals to pursue
    happiness in all that you do
I wish for you to have
    beautiful experiences
    each new day
    as you follow your dreams

                        ~ Susan Polis Schutz

Thank You, Mom

Thank you for providing me with the stability
to keep me confident
the knowledge to help me accomplish things
the strength to help me conquer difficulties
the dedication to help me grow
and the enormous amount of time that you spend
to keep us close
Thank you for always being there to help
for always being there to understand
and for always being there to care
You are a very rare person
because you put your family's needs
    far ahead of your own
I want you to know
how much I appreciate everything you do
I want to thank you
for being such an important and beautiful person
in our family
and I want you to know that you can
depend on me
for anything that you might need
I love you more
than anything in the world

∾Susan Polis Schutz

Thank You, Daughter

I've been so proud of you throughout the years. With exquisite joy and delight, I have watched you grow and marveled at the mysteries and curiosities of each stage unraveling before my eyes. You've made me so happy; your love has kept me solid through my own journey in life.

I look at you now, Daughter, and see such beauty in the woman you are becoming, and I'm so glad that you've stayed close to me. It means so much when you ask for my advice or opinion on things. We have a mutual respect for each other that continues to strengthen.

You have enriched my life more than you'll ever know, and you have taught me so much about being a parent, a mom, a friend... and a person. I love you, and I'm so very proud of you. Please know that no matter where you may be or where you will go, I'll be right there with you... in a special place in your heart.

∽Debbie Burton-Peddle

The love we share
as mother and daughter
is a bond of the strongest kind.
It is a love of the present,
interwoven with memories
of the past
and dreams of the future.
It is strengthened by
    overcoming obstacles and
facing fears and challenges together.
It is having pride in each other
and knowing that our love
can withstand anything.
It is sacrifice and tears,
laughter and hugs.
It is understanding, patience,
and believing in each other.

It is wanting only the best
for each other
and wanting to help anytime
there is a need.
It is respect, a hug,
and unexpected kindness.
It is making time to be together
and knowing just what to do and say.
It is an unconditional,
forever kind of love.

～ Barbara Cage

Mothers and Daughters Are Gifts to Each Other for Life

Mothers and daughters have a bond of closeness that will never break — a friendship that's unconditional between two never-ending friends. They are closer than any two best friends. One is always looking up to the other, and both are looking out for the other. They are perfect listeners, helpers, advisers, hopers, honesty brokers, promise keepers, and dream sharers. The love between them is proof of love's power.

∽ Donna Fargo

The love between
a mother and daughter
exists in a special place...
where "always" always lasts
and "forever"
never goes away.

∽Laurel Atherton

Acknowledgments continued...

We gratefully acknowledge the permission granted by the following authors, publishers, and authors' representatives to reprint poems or excerpts from their publications. Kelly Maureen Paquet for "Even now, my first thought...." Copyright © 2010 by Kelly Maureen Paquet. All rights reserved. Nicole Cook for "To the Strongest Soul I Know... My Mom." Copyright © 2010 by Nicole Cook. All rights reserved. Laura Medley for "As mother and daughter, we've always been...." Copyright © 2010 by Laura Medley. All rights reserved. Barbara Cage for "Even when my daughter was just...." Copyright © 2010 by Barbara Cage. All rights reserved. Amy L. Kuo for "To My Incredible Daughter." Copyright © 2010 by Amy L. Kuo. All rights reserved. Delacorte Press, a division of Random House, Inc., for "When I stopped seeing..." from MY MOTHER/MY SELF by Nancy Friday. Copyright © 1977 by Nancy Friday. All rights reserved. Kayla Washko for "As a child, I played tea party...." Copyright © 2010 by Kayla Washko. All rights reserved. Peggy Morris for "I love it when people tell me...." Copyright © 2010 by Peggy Morris. All rights reserved. Barbara J. Hall for "I see my heritage in her...." Copyright © 2010 by Barbara J. Hall. All rights reserved. Seal Press, an imprint of Avalon Publishing Group, Incorporated, for "[My daughters have] learned from each other..." by Amy Bloom and "Becoming a mother, having a girl..." by Martha Brockenbrough from IT'S A GIRL: WOMEN WRITERS ON RAISING DAUGHTERS, edited by Andrea J. Buchanan. Copyright © 2006 by Andrea J. Buchanan. All rights reserved. *Celebrity Baby Scoop*, www.celebritybabyscoop.com, for "For me, being a mother of girls..." by Rebecca Romijn from "Rebecca Romijn: Being a Mother of Girls Has Softened Me" by Jenny (*Celebrity Baby Scoop*: June 1, 2010). Copyright © 2010 by *Celebrity Baby Scoop*. All rights reserved. Signe Hammer for "Mothers of daughters are..." from MOTHERS AND DAUGHTERS. Copyright © 1976 by Signe Hammer. All rights reserved. Nicole Sullivan for "I am my mother's daughter...." Copyright © 2010 by Nicole Sullivan. All rights reserved. Villard Books, a division of Random House, Inc., for "When the nurse..." from LOVE CAN BUILD A BRIDGE by Naomi Judd. Copyright © 1993 by Naomi Judd. All rights reserved. *Today's Parent*, www.todaysparent.com, for "We all hope to feel our mother's arm..." from "Parent Time: Mothers & Daughters" by Cathie Kryczka (*Today's Parent*: November 15, 2001). Copyright © 2001 by Cathie Kryczka. All rights reserved. Kathryn Leibovich for "We haven't always agreed on everything...." Copyright © 2010 by Kathryn Leibovich. All rights reserved. Lynda Field for "Even as a little girl...." Copyright © 2010 by Lynda Field. All rights reserved. Mia Geiger for "Some moms have the ability...." Copyright © 2010 by Mia Geiger. All rights reserved. Random House, Inc., for "The moment I held her in my arms..." by Susan Cheever from MOMMY WARS, edited by Leslie Morgan Steiner. Copyright © 2006 by Leslie Morgan Steiner. All rights reserved. Linda E. Knight for "All the little things..." and "Mothers and Daughters Light the World with Their Love." Copyright © 2010 by Linda E. Knight. All rights reserved. Jacqueline Schiff for "Family is the bridge across time..." and "What My Mother Has Given to Me." Copyright © 2010 by Jacqueline Schiff. All rights reserved. *Redbook* for "If she hadn't been there..." by Marlo Thomas (*Redbook*: February 1977). Copyright © 1977 by *Redbook*. All rights reserved. Rachel Carrere for "A Mother's Lullaby." Copyright © 2010 by Rachel Carrere. All rights reserved. Dianne Cogar for "How quickly she went from...." Copyright © 2010 by Dianne Cogar. All rights reserved. Conari Press, an imprint of Red Wheel/Weiser, www.redwheelweiser.com, for "At first you take care of your daughter's every need..." from BETWEEN MOTHER & DAUGHTER by Judy Ford and Amanda Ford. Copyright © 1999 by Judy Ford and Amanda Ford. All rights reserved. Linda C. Tuttle for "For My Grown-Up Daughter." Copyright © 2010 by Linda C. Tuttle. All rights reserved. City Lights Foundation Books for "For a Daughter Who Leaves" from LOVE WORKS by Janice Mirikitani. Copyright © 2003 by Janice Mirikitani. All rights reserved. Pam Brown for "You never realize how much...." Copyright © 2010 by Pam Brown. All rights reserved. Machella D. Fisher for "There was a time when she needed me...." Copyright © 2010 by Machella D. Fisher. All rights reserved. Johnson Publishing Company for "Mother and daughter" from "Mothers and Daughters: The Special Connection" by Laura B. Randolph (*Ebony*: February 1988). Copyright © 1988 by Johnson Publishing Company. All rights reserved. Suzy Toronto for "My Mother, My Mirror." Copyright © 2010 by Suzy Toronto. All rights reserved. Linda Sackett-Morrison for "Throughout the day, Daughter, I offer...." Copyright © 2010 by Linda Sackett-Morrison. All rights reserved. PrimaDonna Entertainment Corp. for "Mothers and Daughters Are Gifts to Each Other for Life" by Donna Fargo. Copyright © 2008 by PrimaDonna Entertainment Corp. All rights reserved.

A careful effort has been made to trace the ownership of selections used in this anthology in order to obtain permission to reprint copyrighted material and give proper credit to the copyright owners. If any error or omission has occurred, it is completely inadvertent, and we would like to make corrections in future editions provided that written notification is made to the publisher:

BLUE MOUNTAIN ARTS, INC., P.O. Box 4549, Boulder, Colorado 80306.